SELF-DISCIPLINE
FOR KIDS

Kids will learn, catch them young

Deborah G. Nichols

LEGAL NOTICE

Table of Contents

Foreword

CHAPTER 1:

BASICS OF DISCIPLINE
    The Fundamentals of Discipline

CHAPTER 2

CONSIDER WHERE YOUR CHILD STRUGGLES
    Where Help Is Needed

CHAPTER 3

USE AGE APPROPRIATE CONSEQUENCES
    The Right Discipline
    10 Healthy Discipline Strategies That Work

CHAPTER 4

BE CLEAR ABOUT EXPECTATIONS AND CONSEQUENCES
    Beating and Harsh Words are Harmful and Don't Work. Here's Why:
    Make it Clear

SECTION 5:

WHAT AMOUNT OF WARNING IS ENOUGH?
    Just A Single Time
    Not Fitting The Discipline To Your Kid

CHAPTER 6:

WHEN TO BE CONSISTENT OR GIVE UP
    Continue Onward

FINAL NOTE

Foreword

Everybody needs to have some type of discipline implanted into their lives to make a perfection that will assist the individual with working in an OK way. The greater part of these discipline components are taken from an extremely youthful age and for the most part started by the guardians of the youngster. To show the youngster how to ultimately reproduce into society and be sensible, these discipline measures are essential.

CHAPTER 1:

BASICS OF DISCIPLINE

Summary

Coming up next are a portion of the fundamental discipline ways of thinking that are typically acquainted with a kid from an extremely youthful age.

Discipline is the design that assists the child with squeezing into this present reality joyfully and actually. It is the establishment for the advancement of the child's own self-restraint. Powerful and positive discipline is tied in with educating and directing children, not simply constraining them to comply. Likewise with any remaining intercessions pointed toward calling attention to an inadmissible way of behaving, the child ought to constantly realize that the parent loves and supports the person in question. Trust among parent and child ought to be kept up with and continually based upon.

Nurturing is the assignment of bringing up children and giving them the vital material and close to home consideration to additional their physical, profound, mental and social turn of events.

Training children is one of the most significant yet troublesome obligations of nurturing, and there are no alternate routes. The doctor should be pressured that showing limits and satisfactory conduct takes time and a lot of energy. The rushed speed of the present society can be an obstruction to powerful trains.

The objective of viable discipline is to encourage satisfactory and suitable conduct in the child and to raise genuinely mature grown-ups. A trained individual can delay joy, is obliging of the necessities of others, is self-assured without being forceful or threatening, and can endure distress when fundamental.

The underpinning of powerful discipline is regard. The child ought to have the option to regard the parent's power and furthermore the privileges of others. Irregularity in applying discipline won't assist a child with regards to their folks. Cruel discipline like embarrassment (obnoxious attack, yelling, ridiculing) will likewise make it difficult for the child to regard and trust the parent.

The Fundamentals of Discipline

Great discipline isn't tied in with working out disciplines, as this does not actually show the child the real pessimism of the demonstration that required some discipline consideration. Rather it truly shows the child that the more grounded part in the condition normally gets to direct and make the more vulnerable one essentially track.

Great discipline measures are intended to show a child right from wrong also, not basic location, some unacceptable. Causing the child to grasp self control and a socially OK way of behaving is one approach to empowering the strategy for great discipline.

The parent will show understanding of appropriate conduct with adulation and support and will generally address awful ways of behaving with the valuable chance to teach utilizing admiration, persistence and great issue addressing ability instead of basically figuring out discipline.

Great discipline isn't tied in with going through the course of a power battle. At the point when a child is a lot more youthful it might appear to be satisfactory to utilize this sort of discipline yet as the child becomes older it would be significantly more challenging to involve this style as the more seasoned child will more possible fight back, in this way exacerbating the all around tough spot.

Great discipline doesn't mean causing the child to feel offended or using disparaging components to cause hurt. Utilizing styles like shouting and verbally abusing won't help the child in any certain manner.

CHAPTER 2

CONSIDER WHERE YOUR CHILD STRUGGLES

Summary

Each child has issues in specific regions in their lives which might cause some disciplinary prerequisite for these issues not to heighten wild. Anyway it isn't generally straightforward the child's situation and issue and working out some type of discipline without an exhaustive comprehension will just exacerbate the situation.

Understanding.your child is perhaps the main thing that you ought to advance as a parent. It is extremely useful in becoming viable in directing and supporting your child as they develop and develop. You really want to remember that your child has a special character quality that stays reliable over the course of life.

One of the manners in which you can comprehend your child is by noticing them as they rest, eat, or play. Search for reliable characteristics. Which exercises do they like best? Is acclimating to changes simple for them or do they require time to get comfortable with these things? These things are the ordinary qualities of a child and your child may not be a special case.

However much as could be, have opportunity and energy to converse with your children as this is vital to acquiring data and understanding. On account of small kids, they require less verbal language and more look and non-verbal communication to figure out their viewpoints and sentiments. Asking them inquiries will permit them to talk about their thoughts to you.

Where Help Is Needed

Frequently children will imitate what they have seen from those nearest to them, consequently a large portion of the battles a child encounters willin the long run be addressed the manner they see the guardians or grown-ups around the do as such.

Accordingly in the journey to help out the child through the issues and the strategies utilized for appropriate arrangements, each
thought ought to be given to downplaying why the child has an issue in a specific region to begin with. Coming up next are a portion of the manners in which that can be taken on when working out discipline while as yet being exceptionally mindful of the areas the child battles in:

Choose how to deal with the circumstance without further adding to the problem. Make strides that would build up discipline yet at the equivalent time the strategy utilized ought to likewise permit the child to comprehend and acknowledge things are being finished, taking their wellbeing to heart.

Utilizing immovability yet salting it with generosity will go far in assuring the child that the parent figures out the battle, yet does not approve the way of behaviour being displayed with respect to the child. Supporting through supporters might appear like a weird concept to follow however will be powerful over the long haul as it doesn't mean to bring down the child's normal soul and pizzazz.

Having family meetings to resolve the issue will likewise serve to show the child that their sentiments and battles are being thought of and mean quite a bit to all. This will assist the child with tolerating the discipline measures with less possibilities of insubordination.

CHAPTER 3

USE AGE APPROPRIATE CONSEQUENCES

Summary

To train a child appropriately, there ought to preferably be an idea given to how the parent ought to approach the activity and what kind of activity ought to be thought of. Just working out discipline for restraining a child won't be useful by any means and may here and there try and have a horrendous outcome.

Frequently parents fail to remember that the purpose in training kids is to give them firm rules and cutoff points so they needn't bother with being rebuffed. Training implies defining up limits and assumptions so that children realize what is expected of them. The essential objective is to have children figure out how to ultimately direct themselves so they needn't bother with being rebuffed.

The Right Discipline

Coming up next are a few rules that can assist with settling on the decision of discipline measure more proper to both the child's age and to address the demonstration that necessary the discipline is a reasonably corresponding and fitting way:

The parent ought to consider the improvement stage the child is going through. This ought to be on a singular premise as this may differ enormously even in a similar age bunch. Understanding books and other material on this might be useful in steering the parent in the correct heading. Begin constructing a solid groundwork for standards of conduct. Guarantee the child comprehends from an early age what is OK and what not adequate way of behaving is.

Managing this before there is really a need to address any inappropriate conduct by working out disciplinary activity will be better for the child as the child won't be confounded by the abrupt invasion of the negative response from the parent. Understanding mental health overall is additionally significant as it is vital that children have the option to grasp the disciplinary action taken and not see it as typically awful and inappropriate.

The parent ought to have the option to comprehend that at particular ages the child will respond to things in a specific way that is out of their own cognizance, subsequently the need to comprehend the cerebrum development processes before really figuring out discipline.

Submitting to something that they can truly grasp will be difficult for the child.

10 Healthy Discipline Strategies That Work

Here are a few hints on the most effective ways to assist your child with learning an OK way of behaving as they develop.

They suggested positive discipline techniques that successfully help children to deal with their way of behaving and keep them from getting hurt while advancing a sound turn of events. These include:

1. **Sharing Time**. Show children right from amiss with quiet words and activities. Model ways of behaving you might want to find in your children.

2. **Put Down Certain Boundaries**. Have clear and reliable standards your children can adhere to. Make certain to make sense of these principles in age-fitting terms they can comprehend.

3. **Give Outcomes**. Smoothly and solidly make sense of the outcomes in the event that they don't act. For instance, let her know that if she doesn't get her toys, you will take care of them until the end of the day. Be ready to finish immediately. Try not to give in by giving them back following a couple of moments. Be that as it may, recall, never remove something your child really needs, like a dinner.

4. **Listen To Them**. Listening is significant. Allow your child to complete the story prior to taking care of the issue. Watch for times when bad conduct has an example, as in the event that your child is feeling desirous. Talk with your child about this as opposed to simply giving outcomes.

5. **Truly Focus On Them**. The most incredible asset for successful discipline is consideration — to support great ways of behaving and beat others down. Keep in mind, all children need their parent's consideration.

6. **Find Them Being Great**. Children need to know when they accomplish something awful - and when they accomplish something great. Notice acceptable conduct and point it out, lauding achievement and great attempts. Be explicit (for instance, "Goodness, you worked really hard putting that toy away!").

7. **Know When Not To Answer**. However long your child isn't accomplishing something hazardous and gets a lot of consideration for good ways of behaving, overlooking terrible ways of behaving can be a successful approach to halting it. Overlooking awful ways of behaving can likewise show children regular outcomes of their activities. For instance, assuming your child continues to drop her treats deliberately, she will before long have no more treats left to eat. On the off chance that she tosses and breaks her toy, she can not play with it. It won't be some time before she learns not to drop her treats and to play cautiously with her toys.

8. **Be Ready For Inconvenience**. Prepare for circumstances when your child could experience difficulty acting. Set them up for impending exercises and how you believe that they should act.

9. **Divert Terrible Way Of Behaving**. At times children make trouble since they are exhausted or don't have the foggiest idea about any better. Find something different for your child to do.

10. **Get Down On A Period**. A break can be particularly valuable when a particular rule is broken. This discipline device works best by advance notice children they will get a break in the event that they don't quit, reminding them what they fouled up in as few words—and with as little emotion—as conceivable, and eliminating them from the circumstance for a pre-set timeframe (1 moment each extended period old enough is a decent guideline). With children who are no less than 3 years of age, you can have a go at allowing their children to lead their own break as opposed to setting a clock. You can simply express, "Go to break and return when you feel prepared and in

charge." This system, which can help the child acquire and rehearse self-administration abilities, additionally functions admirably for more seasoned children and adolescents.

CHAPTER 4

BE CLEAR ABOUT EXPECTATIONS AND CONSEQUENCES

Summary

The main thing a parent ought to comprehend is that children are not conceived in a flash knowing all principles and guidelines throughout everyday life. They will advance generally through experimentation and it is the obligation of the parent to show these, in the most effective way conceivable ideally without causing any harm to the child intellectually or genuinely.

Beating and Harsh Words are Harmful and Don't Work. Here's Why:

"Viable Discipline to Raise Healthy Children," features why it means a lot to zero in on showing acceptable conduct as opposed to rebuffing a terrible way of behaving. Research shows that beating, slapping and different types of actual discipline don't function admirably to address a child's way of behaving. Similar turns out as expected for hollering at or disgracing a child. Past being incapable, brutal physical and verbal disciplines can likewise harm a child's drawn out physical and emotional well-being.

Hitting's Undesirable Cycle. Rather than showing liability and restraint, beating frequently builds hostility and outrage in children. An investigation of children brought into the world in 20 huge U.S. urban communities found that families who utilized actual discipline got found out in a negative cycle: the more children were punished, the more they later made trouble, which provoked more spankings accordingly. Hitting's belongings may likewise be felt past the parent-child relationship. Since it instructs that causing somebody torment is OK assuming you're baffled — even with those you love. Children who are hit might be bound to hit others when they don't get what they need.

Enduring Imprints. Actual discipline builds the gamble of injury, particularly in children under a year and a half old enough, and may make other quantifiable imprints on the cerebrum and body. Children who are hit show more elevated levels of chemicals attached to harmful pressure. Actual discipline may likewise influence mental health. One investigation discovered that youthful grown-ups who were hit over and again had less dark matter, the piece of the mind engaged with restraint, and performed lower on IQ tests as youthful grown-ups than the benchmark group.

Obnoxious Attack: How words hurt. Shouting at children and utilizing words to cause profound agony or disgrace likewise has been viewed as insufficient and hurtful. Cruel verbal discipline, even by guardians who are generally warm and adoring, can prompt more rowdiness and psychological well-being issues in children. Research shows that unforgiving verbal discipline, which turns out to be more normal as children progress in years, may prompt more conduct issues and side effects of gloom in teenagers.

Make it Clear

Coming up next are a few rules that can assist the parent with understanding how to guarantee the child is clear about the assumptions furthermore, results before there is a requirement for discipline:

The two players ought to have the option to comprehend and acknowledge that the discipline worked out isn't intended to address discipline exclusively
yet, is to assist the child with controlling the need to act with a specific goal in mind from here on out.

This will assist the child with understanding that the discipline or discipline measure taken isn't intended to damage or mischief nor is everything about the power. The thought behind the activity taken ought to plainly show the child the assumptions and outcomes that are straightforwardly connected with a specific demonstration in particular and that's it.

Mistaking the child for non connective components won't assist the child with isolating the different demonstrations and the discipline measure taken particularly in the event that the child is extremely youthful and concerning the more established child, there is the probability of hatred constructing when shamefulness is seen.

The child ought to comprehend that the assumptions for the guardians and grown-ups around, isn't about a fight for control, but about trimming the child for future reenactment into society and making the progress is simple and charming.

Being steady in the disciplinary activities worked out and furthermore going to these lengths as quickly as time permits after the culpable conduct is shown in vital. The more youthful the youngster assumes, the more the move initiated to guarantee the kid figures out an association between the activity and the discipline.

SECTION 5:

WHAT AMOUNT OF WARNING IS ENOUGH?

Summary

Some of the time there is a need to just move away from the genuine need to give out any kind of discipline or disciplinary activity and simply give the youngster a firm admonition. Anyway guardians, who decide to utilize this technique, ought to discover that there ought to likewise be ramifications to be acknowledged and expected should the underlying firm admonition not be stuck to or treated in a serious way.

Just A Single Time

There are multiple ways the firm admonition procedure can work out and this might incorporate a portion of the accompanying manners of thinking:

Regular outcomes - in this specific situation the parent's responsibility is to firmly caution the offspring of particular estimates that ought to be taken for the accommodation of the youngster and on the off chance that these actions are not taken, the parent won't step in and make up for any misfortune or negative events.

The youngster will be instructed that the firm admonition is all the assistance the individual in question will get and should work with the consequences of their activities.

Intelligent outcomes - this is one more way the parent can handle what is happening with only a firm admonition. Out opportunity to make sense of for the youngster the results of various activities before the kid is gotten in a position where the person in question would need to respond is one approach to being firm, as the parent's clarification ought to in a perfect world likewise incorporate the degree of help not out of the ordinary from the parent and that's it.

This will likewise assist the youngster with settling on choices on exactly the amount they are ready to deal with and in the event that such activities merit the conceivable unfortunate results which they should manage themselves and acknowledge.

Positive discipline - here the parent won't just make sense of the results however will guarantee the youngster that the outcomes will be worked out with practically no expectation of give and take.

Not Fitting The Discipline To Your Kid

With regards to child discipline, one size doesn't fit all. What dealt with a youngster's kin or the children of companions might be some unacceptable methodology for a kid. More than once attempting to utilize a specific way to deal with right or guide a youngster's way of behaving probably won't turn out best for a singular kid.

The Fix: Remember that kids, similar to grown-ups, have their own characters, dispositions, and peculiarities. One youngster might be more difficult than others or be bound to have an implosion when things don't turn out well for them. Attempt various ways to deal with tailor discipline procedures to every individual youngster.

For example, while one kid might have the option to concentrate and quit dallying after a couple of general updates, another youngster might require outlines, timetables, and closer oversight to keep them on target.

One child might quit getting rowdy after an advance notice that they will lose honors (a toy or a movement), while another kid may really have to have those things removed and experience the results of terrible way of behaving before they figure out how to observe the guidelines,

CHAPTER 6:

WHEN TO BE CONSISTENT OR GIVE UP

Summary

Supporter is truly difficult for a parent to take an interest reliably in particularly when the parent is either as a rule never around or when the youngster is sufficiently cunning to appear to be blameless when the ideal opportunity for restraining comes around.

Continue Onward

Anyway guardians ought to figure out that all discipline ought to have some structure on consistency, to be successful on any level. There is likewise the significance of causing the kid to comprehend this demeanour of consistency so the person will comprehend that each activity has a resulting response be it sure or negative.

In the event that the guardians can be steady and hold fast no matter what, the kids will before long get familiar with the significance of weighting their activities before really following up on them. This will ultimately make things simpler for both parent and kid. Being reliable and relentless in the discipline region will likewise help the more youthful youngster comprehend the specific way of behaving or activity isn't going to be endured and hence will gradually wean themselves off.

Anyway in the event that the discipline isn't reliable the youngster will figure out how to move what is going on as per the parent's emotional episodes hence showing them how to get their direction cleverly. Other than this the youngster will likewise be extremely confused when the disciplinary activity isn't predictable and the youngster can not actually grasp the hugeness of the negative demonstration if the discipline worked out contrasts extensively each time.

Attempting various kinds of discipline to make the youngster comprehend the negative demonstration is unsuitable is okay yet the disciplinary activity worked out ought to be along comparative lines of seriousness so consistency can be actually kept up with consistently. For the parent, keeping to this consistency will likewise make their work a lot simpler and unsurprising and this is a significant component to consolidate in the child's psyche.

FINAL NOTE

In the event that the kid is too youthful to even think about understanding to method of discipline being given out, the disarray won't permit the youngster to as a matter of fact center around the negative demonstration that caused the requirement for discipline however will make the youngster center around the way that perhaps the parent doesn't actually cherish or really focus on them all things considered. This is exceptionally harming for a small kid and can have extensive impacts that are perhaps so implanted in their subliminal that it might be challenging to change.

Inaccurate discipline may likewise make the youngster feel second rate and along these lines in the long run become exceptionally removed. This may likewise disintegrate their confidence.

A youngster with low confidence issues will likewise wind up having issues in different pieces of their life, along these lines making significantly more issues over the long haul.
In the event that the supporter for the most part takes on an actual mode, the youngster
will ultimately learn or see the best way to get what they need is to be actual about it.

Wrong type of discipline can likewise cause a youngster to feel angry towards the parent in this way causing grating inside the nuclear family. Some of the time this can bring about relationships going sour.

Printed in Great Britain
by Amazon

44500906R00020